SUPERBASE 14
FORT BRAGG

SUPERBASE 14

FORT BRAGG

America's Airborne Elite

Mike Verier

Published in 1990 by Osprey Publishing Limited
59 Grosvenor Street, London W1X 9DA

British Library Cataloguing in Publication Data
Verier, Mike
  Fort Bragg.
  1. United States, Army Air force.
Military helicopters
  I. Title
  623.74′6047

    ISBN 0–85045–963–X

Editor Dennis Baldry
Designed by Stewart Cocking
Printed in Hong Kong

Front cover Virtually stacked one on top of the other, 82nd Airborne paratroopers depart the smoky C-141 Starlifter for *terra firma* far below

Back cover As soon as the wheels touch the ground the infantry race down the tail ramp of the Chinook and dive into the prone position. Tactical considerations aside, lying down is probably the safest thing to do when the CH-47 moves

Title pages As the sun inches over the horizon the EH-60 lowers its distinctive aerial

Right The author, trusty F-1 at the ready, prepares for a photo-sortie with Karl Ebert. The wind-proofing is necessary because even with the sun shining it's a mite draughty in the back of a doorless OH-58

Far right If you know Fort Bragg you'll know that this is 'Iron Mike', sculpted by Leah Heibert, wife of a former deputy post chaplain. The 15 foot bronze depicting the classic Airborne soldier of the World War 2 stands ever vigilant, and more than anything else symbolizes the Airborne spirit—proud of their history but always looking forward and alert for any call

Acknowledgements

This book would not have been possible without the enthusiastic co-operation of Fort Bragg itself. Everyone, from general to private soldier was unfailingly tolerant of the author's sometimes strange requests. Every photographer will know that the quality of the pictures is in direct proportion to the quality of access afforded. In this case I couldn't possibly have had more support. There are many anonymous individuals who gave their time willingly, and to all these men and women I give my heartfelt thanks. Particular thanks to the following:–
XVIII Airborne Corps: Lt Col David R Kiernan, Major Baxter Ennis and Sgts Cordell and Arden.
82nd Airborne: Capt Mike Phillips for the kind loan of his office, Capt Diedre Cozzens, who froze in the back of an OH-58 on our behalf, the unfailingly helpful Sergeant Jacson for the splendid targets of opportunity, and Specialist Cooley for the memorable cross-country in a 'Humm Vee'!

Others include Capt Hammond and 1st Sgt Spain of Alpha CO 3/73rd Armour, Jim Isbell and Frank Ketchie of ABNSOTB, pilots CW3 Joe F Pearson for allowing me to join the Chinook lift exercise, and Capt Karl M Ebert whose understanding of photographic requirements has resulted in some of the best pictures within these pages. Also Richard Calder of the London Embassy Press Office, Tom Kolk and Bryan Wilburn, Dennis, Cathy and Tony (the A team), Canon UK, and the Public Affairs Office at Pope AFB. Finally very special thanks to Randy Jolly for providing spare film at a critical moment!

All the photos were taken with Canon lenses mounted on F-1 and T-90 bodies. Film was Kodak 64 and 200 transparency throughout.

One last word. Fort Bragg is an 'open' base and includes several excellent museums and places of historical interest which anyone can visit. Access to flight-lines, ranges and training areas, however, was only possible with extensive prior clearance. You are not advised to point cameras at things military without this!

Introduction

17th December 1903: a cold morning at a desolate windswept place known as Kill Devil Hill, near Kitty Hawk, North Carolina. Here Orville Wright was to make man's first faltering powered flight of just 120 feet. Half a century earlier the American Civil War had raged across the same area, briefly bringing to notice a confederate general and native North Carolinian, Braxton Bragg.

These two apparently unconnected facts bear a direct influence on this book. In August 1918 the Army, in search of somewhere to train the men needed for World War 1, established Camp Bragg and seven months later, in March 1919, a permanent flying facility was established right next door to the growing camp. Pope Field was named after a young lieutenant killed whilst flying a JN-4 Jenny less than two months earlier. Pope AFB (which it became on the separation of the Air Force from the old Army Air Corps in 1948) is today the oldest active airfield in the inventory. In 1922 Camp Bragg was designated a permanent installation and became Fort Bragg. Less than two decades later the 82nd was one of five divisions trained at Fort Bragg for the parachute role. Here the Airborne was created and thus history has inextricably linked aviation, the Army, and North Carolina.

Today, the two facilities have merged into one vast military area, with each part totally dependent on the other for its mission. So big is the area that virtually any road north out of nearby Fayetteville takes you there. In case you're in any doubt as to your destination, the roads have names like 'Bragg Boulevard' and 'The All American Freeway'. The 'gee whiz' statistics are breathtaking: two airfields (Pope and Simmonds), miles of roads, paths, tank tracks, acres of drop zones and training areas. Home to nearly 40,000 active duty soldiers, Bragg actually supports some 172,000 people by the time civilian employees and families are counted. Its primary occupants are the 82nd Airborne. Part of the XVIII Airborne Corps, which is also headquartered at Bragg, the 82nd is unique in many ways, not least that it is the only Airborne division still 'in role' as paratroops (all other 'airborne' divisions are

'airmobile' and stay in their aircraft until they've landed). Part of the Rapid Deployment Force, their mission is very simple—go anywhere in the World at no notice, go in first, and WIN! Whilst the actual mission requirement is to be wheels up and en-route within 18 hours they can do much better—Grenada was accomplished in 10. The Division is divided into nine sections and rotated through an alert status running from one to nine. On alert level one (which can last for six weeks) you keep your bags packed and stay within earshot of a phone. Moreover *everyone* goes. Cooks, clerks or generals, male or female, every soldier in the 82nd is jump-qualified. The Division is completely self-contained, with its own armour, artillery, aviation and support elements, all of which can deploy or be transported by air.

But what of the people? There is no doubting that this is an elite formation. Motivation and morale is high, re-enlistment a frequently taken option, and they also have a strong sense of identity. Everywhere you go is redolant with history; roads are named after famous battles, and the British red beret is worn with pride. Nor are the men and women of the 82nd the 'gung ho' types so beloved of popular fiction—they are intelligent professionals who know that if history proves one thing it is that freedom must occasionally be fought for.

The mere fact that they can reach out anywhere in the world may itself deter potential aggressors. As a civilian, however, I was reminded during this assignment that the price of freedom is still eternal vigilance, and this author for one is greatly reassured that so precious a commodity lies in the hands of such committed individuals. Airborne!

Right 06–30 on Ardennes. Every morning, rain or shine, the 82nd goes jogging. Irrespective of rank, if you're not engaged on some other duty you run. Each unit, complete with distinctive running strip and guidon bearers, chants its way up and down Ardennes Road which runs for a couple of miles through the divisional area. They round that off with some exercises and then to go work. These men and women are *fit*

Contents

All the way with the Double-A

Below With flaps down a C-141 Starlifter passes over the deployed parachutes from the last drop as its own run begins. The side doors are normally used to drop two 'sticks' of soldiers. The first two are out and the next is just clearing the doorway

Left A few moments later and troopers are spilling into the sky. From this picture you can clearly see just how quickly the static-line parachutes deploy. This is essential to ensure that the lowest possible altitude is used, thus minimising the soldiers' vulnerable moments under the nylon

The six C-141s used for this drop can be seen smoking their way home as the sky over Drop Zone (DZ) Sicily fills with parachutes. The Starlifter in its stretched form can carry up to 168 paratroops, all of whom can be deployed in seconds. The last aircraft has just disgorged its load whilst the first soldiers are already on the ground

Once down, the first job is to secure the area and link up with the vehicles and heavy equipment which arrived (as we shall see) a few moments ahead of the first jumper

Green Ramp at Pope AFB. Airborne soldiers of the 82nd prepare for the jump you have just seen. The maroon beret originated with the British forces during World War II, and has since become the international symbol of airborne troops. Royal Artillery red was worn unofficially until 1979 when officialdom attempted to do away with such distinctions. This intolerable situation was corrected in 1980 when the Army officially recognised the colour and re-issued the berets to the Division. The announcement of this fact by Maj Gen GS Meloy to a packed Towle stadium reportedly produced a roar of approval that rocked the structure

Fully rigged with T-10B parachute and weapons/equipment containers, the men do what they can to make themselves comfortable in the heat. These men are wearing the now standard 'fritz' kevlar helmet. At first regarded with some suspicion, the 'plastic' helmet has proven its worth in combat. Housed in the regimental museum is an example brought back from Grenada by its grateful (and unscathed) owner that has an AK-47 round still lodged in it

A rigger makes a final check on the reserve chute whilst the Starlifters, living up to their 'lizard' paint job, bask in the sun. Just behind them can be seen the tails of the Hercules that will drop the heavy equipment

Left An HMMWV hits Sicily. The parachute lines have just been cut by explosive guillotines and the canopies will drop clear of the load. Framed by the collapsing parachutes, the following Hercules bore in with their loads

Above Immediately above the camera a pallet containing a Deuce-and-a-half swings beneath its rapidly blossoming canopy

Whump! As the aforementioned truck impacts the DZ and sheds its shroud lines the sharp-eyed will detect the author's camera case inside the shadow of a collapsing parachute to the right of the picture. Tactical withdrawal from this otherwise excellent camera position was deemed prudent at the time. Over in minutes, this type of arrival would normally be carried out at night just to make it more interesting. It is, of course, impossible to convey in photographs the drama and excitement of a full scale parachute assault, but the author was left in no doubt that it remains the fastest, and indeed only way to insert men and equipment into a precise location, which could be literally anywhere in the world

Having deposited the author on Sicily, the intrepid Karl Ebert in his photo OH-58 prepares to make his escape before it starts raining tanks. The nimble OH-58 is used extensively for a variety of tasks ranging from liaison and scouting to more aggressive roles

Below The CH-47D Chinook—known in British services as the 'wokka'—equips the 18th Aviation Brigade and provides the 82nd with its heavy lifting ability. Featuring a triple hook external load system, more powerful engines and composite blades, the Delta offers considerable improvements over earlier models. Here CW3 Joe Pearson and his co-pilot run through the checks on the Simmonds ramp. His helmet is equipped for night-vision goggles. The circular orange instrument is the display for the radar warning receiver which tells the pilot where hostile emissions originate, and what is emitting them. This is a real attention-grabber when you are being followed by a target as big as Chinook

Right The first aircraft pauses briefly on the LZ as number two comes in for his pick-up

Having collected an infantry squad
we go looking for a dirt road with a
HMMWV parked on it

Framed by the rapidly closing ramp, we depart the area. As soon as the Chinook is clear the men on the ground will sprint to the HMMWV and prepare to hook it onto the second aircraft which is just visible a little further down the road

Soldiers wearing NBC (Nuclear, Biological, Chemical) masks prepare to hook the load to the Chinook. An earth line attached to a pole is first touched to the airframe as the static charge built up by so much moving machinery is considerable

Below As the Chinook eases down into the Landing Zone (LZ) a crewman cranes out of the side door to check rotor clearance. The downwash from the twin rotors creates a huge dust storm every time the CH-47 nears the ground, hence the helicopter's nickname 'Big Windy'

Right Up and out of the LZ, the load, complete with its helicopter, heads for the dirt road again

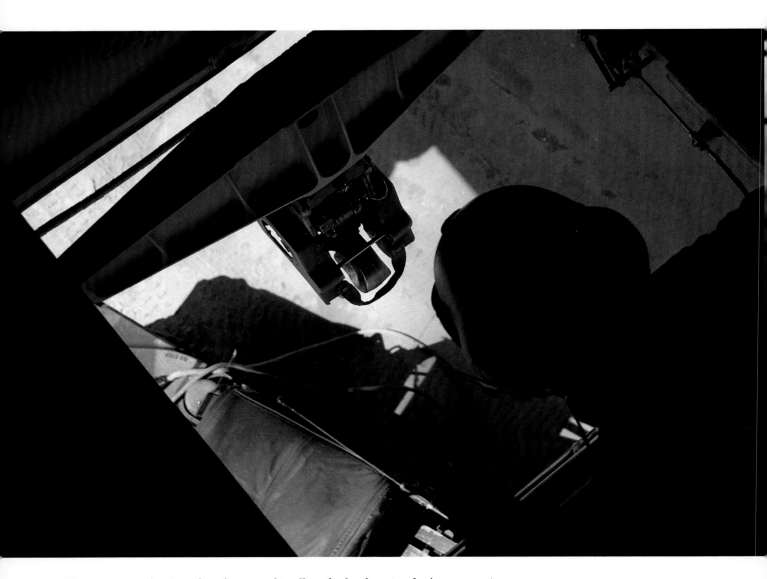

The centre section trap door is opened to allow the loadmaster, laying prone, to supervise the hook-up. He will feed precise instructions to the pilot who cannot see what's going on underneath the aircraft. The hook is mounted on a transverse beam which is free to swing fore and aft, thus preventing at least some of the load movement from affecting the aircraft

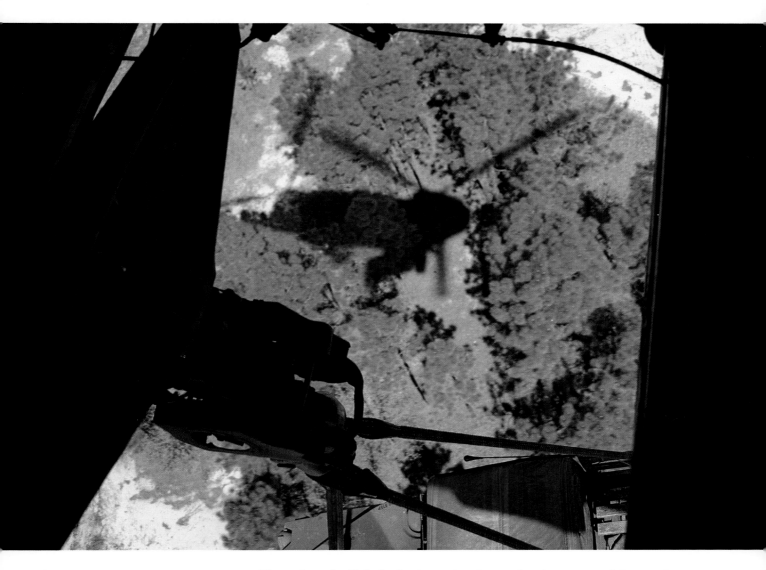

Throughout the flight the load remains close to the pine trees and dogwoods that characterize North Carolina (this is tactical flying at its best). Carrying an underslung load is very demanding because the load and the helicopter behave as two pendulums connected by a length of elastic. What this means is that sudden control movement will result in the load flying the aircraft. Technically, it is referred to as 'pilot induced oscillation' and if it is not damped very quickly the only solution is to jettison the load—clearly not something to enhance your standing in the crewroom

The All Americans' speciality is the airfield take-down, which is accomplished by the traditional parachute assault. Very close behind them, however, will be the Black Hawks, either flown in by C-5 Galaxy or self-deployed

Left Sikorsky's ubiquitous UH-60 has earned itself a reputation as a tough and reliable replacement for the trusty Huey. The type's baptism of fire with the 82nd came in Grenada where it proved capable of absorbing considerable battle damage. The physically small, but impressively powerful twin General Electric T700 engines give the UH-60 greater safety margins, more lifting capability and a much higher speed

Above A Black Hawk delivers a 105 mm howitzer and its crew to an LZ. This is accomplished with impressive speed and the gun can be firing less than a minute after the helicopter clears the zone

The gun in question, officially the M-102, belongs to C battery, 3rd Btn 319th Airborne Field Artillery, a unit founded in 1917 and one that has been a part of the 82nd ever since. The mobility of this elite unit is truly remarkable, as is their rate of fire.

The second round is in the air before the first has landed, and the battery can be packed and on the move again before the enemy has time to respond. Prime mover for the 105 is the versatile HMMWV which too can be airlifted by the UH-60

Capable of firing a round every six seconds out to a range of nearly 12 km (further with rocket assisted munitions), the gunners can give an adversary a considerable headache

Left Two at a time means that a whole battalion (18 guns) can be quickly airlifted wherever needed

Above Sometimes the helicopters can't land. No sweat, the paras just abseil down

Right The door-gunner directs soldiers into the UH-60. The exhaust suppression and intake protection measures fitted to the Black Hawk can be clearly seen in this shot. The airframe bulge above the gunner's head covers the now standard attachment points for the external stores support system (ESSS) 'wings'

Below Complete with its low-viz crossed sabres, this Black Hawk is configured 'as delivered' and lacks the mods described above. It does however mount the distinctive AN/ALQ 144 'disco lights' IR jammer

Above A pristine UH-60 hover-taxies, hence the 'unloaded' undercarriage

Right Even at a busy airfield like Simmonds it is unusual to see a twelve-ship lift.
In view of this we were granted permission to overfly the runway for this
impressive line-up

The formation arrives at the LZ. Despite the fact that there are still pools of rain on the ground, the North Carolina red dirt soon forms a sand storm

Right Shortly after daybreak on the Simmonds ramp. This machine has both ESSS stub wings fitted and mounts two of the long range tanks that give the aircraft an impressive self-deployment capability. The ESSS is a bolt-on system that can quickly add to the capabilities of this extremely versatile aircraft. The pylons are also capable of mounting armament, and the Black Hawk has been cleared to mount the Rockwell Hellfire air-to-ground missile. However, the Army at present has no plans to use that particular capability

Below Unlike the venerable UH-1 Huey, the UH-60 can be towed around the flight-line with no prior preparation. The chaff/flare dispenser on the rear fuselage is a key part of the helicopters' self-defence capability

Heavy Metal – Lizard, Spectre, and Metal Overcast

Pope's ramp is ample testimony to the versatility of the C-130. This remarkable aeroplane goes quietly about its duties year after year, yet without it half the world's air forces, let alone the 82nd, couldn't move. Capable of delivering men and equipment to the battlefield whether by parachute, or by landing directly onto a minimally prepared strip, the Hercules serves in great numbers and in many forms

Below This one sports an interesting variation on the basic 'Europe One' colour scheme, re-touching adding to the effect

Left Not often seen these days, the Fulton Recovery System was originally developed to lift downed aircrew from the sea or remote land sites. It is also useful for individuals from the Special Forces who might be anxious to depart enemy territory quickly. This aircraft has just collected the wire (visible aft of the open ramp) and the victim on the ground is split seconds away from being yanked almost vertically skywards from a sitting position, with his back to the aircraft—certainly one of the more interesting ways to board an aeroplane

Left A Herc variant of a more aggressive nature is the AC-130E gunship. Although not based at Pope/Fort Bragg, the AC-130 would be used in support of a landing, as was the case in Grenada. Captured during a stopover at Pope, this machine gives some idea of the awesome firepower the AC-130 can unleash

Below The nose art leaves one in no doubt as to the intent of this crew, and indicates the customarily nocturnal habits of this species. Below and to the left is the radome for the Black Crow system, whilst the blast deflector and door cover the 'eyes' of the gunship, the AN/ASQ24A Stabilised Tracking Set which includes Low Level Light TV

Immediately aft of the nose are a pair of 20 mm Vulcans. Derived from the system fitted to the 'Century Series' fighters, the Vulcan is a potent weapon. The 82nd has trailer mounted Vulcans which are used for both anti-aircraft and direct fire roles. To the far right of the picture is the ball turret housing the AN/AAD-7 infra-red detecting set

Further aft, at the other end of the undercarriage sponson, is a 40 mm cannon, and a fully grown artillery piece in the shape of a 105 mm howitzer. Between the two big guns is the beacon tracking radar

Right Having just returned from a drop a Starlifter passes over the threshold at Pope. The C-141B features a considerable stretch in fuselage length from the early A models. This came about because it was found the aircraft would bulk-out well before its maximum weight was reached

Below Wearing the now standard 'European One' scheme which appears on virtually all Military Airlift Command aircraft, a pair of lizard-like C-141Bs bask in the sun as they await take-off clearance. The air-to-air refuelling receptical is housed in the hump above the cockpit

Previously used for the carriage of bulk loads (such as a six-pack of AH-64 Apaches), the mighty C-5 Galaxy has just been qualified for paratroop jumps, demonstrating this capability at the time of the author's visit. The exact number of paratroopers is classified, but readers may be assured that, in common with everything else about the C-5, it is a large figure. There are a mass of 'gee-whizz' statistics about the aircraft, but perhaps the most impressive one of all is that the Wright brothers' first flight (which of course took place in North Carolina) could be accomplished *inside it*. Here the remarkably agile behemoth spirals out of the LZ. Seeing that it may need to operate into and out of an airfield only just secured, and therefore surrounded by hostile forces, the C-5 corkscrew into and out of the LZ well within the airfield's perimeter

By dawn's early light

Below A type which is slowly being supplanted by the AH-64 Apache at Fort Bragg is the AH-1 Cobra. This early morning ramp shot was taken at Simmonds, and features a line of AH-1Es (formerly the AH-1S [ECAS] but since re-designated). This aircraft is fitted with the MILES system which simulates gun and rocket fire with lasers and strobe lights. Interestingly this machine has the tapered K-747 composite rotor, whilst the one behind it has the old 540 metal blade

Left As the sun just clears the horizon we formate on the EH-60 Quick Fix variant whilst flying in an OH-58

Left Another early riser is this OH-58 Kiowa, many versions of which are used by the US Army for duties ranging from utility to armed recce

Above With the frosty landscape below forming an impressive backdrop, the second OH-58 gets in close. It's a lot warmer over there because they haven't got all the doors off

Main picture A few miles away the pilot prepares to drop into the fog bank over Mott Lake. Officially the EH-60 carries the AN/ALQ-151 counter-measures system, and it is this equipment that is referred to as Quick Fix, not the helicopter itself. The system has direction finding and jamming capabilities that far exceed line-of-sight distances, an impressive aspect of the aircraft's performance which has resulted from the Black Hawk's formidable service ceiling of 20,000 feet. Training presents some problems though as one aircraft can blot out every TV set for miles around. From this angle the new exhaust suppressors are very prominent. These combine with chaff/flare dispensers and the AN/ALQ-144 to reduce the risk from infra-red guided missiles

Inset With its aerial now fully deployed, the Quick Fix prepares to depart the area. The gleaming object above the cabin is the ALQ-144 jammer

Right As we descend a few more of the lumps and bumps are revealed. The bulged cover for the ESSS attachment points above the main wheels are clearly visible

Below The fog bank provides a picturesque backdrop for the elegant EH-60

In a rather more natural habitat the EH-60 goes down amongst the trees at the water's edge

These pages and overleaf The EH-60 gradually moves from the shoreline to the centre of the lake, dispersing the mist as it goes. Not normally seen over water, these photos show the considerable footprint made by the rotor downwash.

Below Feet dry, we head back to Simmonds. The Black Hawk's highly effective slab tailplane is a distinctive feature of this successful aircraft

Right With the characteristic red dirt of North Carolina beneath them, the crew of the EH-60 pause for a brief bow before flying off and completing the mission

Two Indians and a snake — all beginning with 'A'

Right Only just de-classified at the time of the author's visit, the original Army Helicopter Improvement Program (AHIP) OH-58 intended solely as a scout for the Apache, has emerged with teeth of its own. Known as the AH-58D, these aircraft have reputedly seen combat in the Gulf. The Saudis have purchased armed AH-58Ds (which differ from the US Army version in not having the mast-mounted sight) following some very tough tests. Whilst results remain classified the prototype returned to Bell's experimental plant with an impressive 'kill' tally on its side which included several Apaches and an S-76

Below A pair of Hellfire missiles give the diminutive AH-58 quite a punch. Both the mounting and the missile are common to the Apache force, helping the Army's supply system considerably

Left The addition of the ubiquitous AN/ALQ 144 jammer, colloquially known in the Army as 'disco lights', has resulted in a somewhat unsightly wart aft of the engine, but it is considered better than collecting a missile in your hot parts. The system is in fact a heat source and works by swamping a missiles' seeker head with confusing returns from its many facets

Right The AH-58 is a very small aircraft indeed. There are so many 'black boxes' in the rear compartment that the aircraft is now only a two seater, and only just at that

Although officially superceded by the Apache, the trusty Cobra is still much in evidence at Simmonds. This line of ECAS airframes (now re-designated AH-1Es) displays an interesting variety of rotor blades

A Cobra is marshalled to its spot past a lugubrious looking Starlifter. In the background a visiting Coast Guard C-130 does its best to brighten up a rather dank afternoon

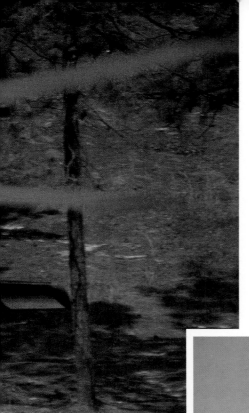

Below It is 08:00 and soon this veteran AH-1 will be airborne to demonstrate to the youngsters (some airframes are now older than their pilots) that there's still only one Cobra. One pilot described the Snake to the author as 'a real sexy aeroplane'—I doubt that there are many Cobra pilots who disagree

Left 'Anything you can do I can do uglier'—the Cobra's replacement, the AH-64A Apache, is now in full scale use with the Division. Faster and meaner than the Snake, it incorporates many of the lessons learnt from flying the Cobra. It also has very advanced sensors. Visible here is the Pilots Night Vision System PNVS, Forward Looking Infra-red (FLIR) ball (the menacing gleam atop the nose) and the Target Acquisition Data System (TADS) in the two-sided turret below it. Combining day and night optics, TV and FLIR with a laser designator and tracker, the TADS/PNVS gives the crews a considerable edge in poor visibility, as is often encountered in 'frontline' Europe.

The last thing you want is a bad guy shooting you down from behind, so the Apache is well defended in both passive and active ways. The dark green paint absorbs radar energy and is non-reflective of both visible and IR light; the hot exhausts are cooled by the massive honeycomb 'black hole' suppressors; and both ends of the turbine are well shielded. If a missile does become locked on to the Apache the crew can still use the infra-red jammer (aft of the rotor pylon) or the chaff/flare dispenser, which is just visible on the lower rear fuselage, immediately ahead of the tailplane

Left Attack helicopter pilots regard themselves as 'fighter' types. The legend on this driver's flight manual pretty well sums up the philosophy. The very distinctive heavy browed helmet worn by Apache crews is also visible, as is the monocle sight which is mounted to it. The device bolted onto the canopy frame above his head is a cable cutter, and behind that can be seen the blade aerial for a radar jammer, another part of the AH-64's defensive suite

Above Out on the arming pad a pair of Apaches are being readied. Here, 30 mm rounds are uploaded for the Hughes chain gun

Right Next the rockets. The unguided 2.7 in folding fin aerial rocket (FFAR) is still a potent helicopter weapon. Great care was needed here as stray voltage, even as small as that emitted by the author's cameras, could fire one of these once armed

Above Safely pointing down-range and nearly ready

Like a great insect the AH-64 tucks its nose down and heads for something to shoot at

Below When in transit, or not required, the TADS/PNVS optics rotate inwards. This protects them from possible damage and removes the possibility of a tell-tale glint betraying the aircraft's position

Right One of the few angles from which the Apache has anything approaching elegance of line. The AH-64 hovers shark-like at the edge of the range

Right Down in the weeds. Army aviators regard the tops of the trees as the upper limit of their airspace. Using clearings little bigger than the rotor disc, an Apache can pop-up, launch a Hellfire, and vanish again in seconds

Overleaf The FFARs are ballistic rockets and can be used as long-range artillery, with remarkable accuracy. Here again a firing position behind the trees is favoured

Green on – go!

Also resident on Fort Bragg is the John F Kennedy Special Warfare Center. The men trained here perform a variety of missions, many of which are of a very sensitive nature. They are specialists and operate in small groups, similar to the SAS. One of their specialities is the HALO (High Altitude Low Opening) parachute landing using advanced steerable canopies. With this technique men can be dropped from great altitude, only opening their parachutes at the last moment to minimise exposure to the enemy. A variation uses high altitude deployment following which the canopy can be 'flown'—albeit somewhat uncomfortably—for thirty miles or more to the target area. Virtually undetectable on radar, this is a true 'stealth' insertion. Given the nature of their work special authorisation had to be obtained to photograph even this training session

Above Yes, it's a CASA 212. No one seems to know how the USAF came by a pair of these Spanish utility types, but they are ideal for the job, with a big rear ramp and ample power to quickly reach altitude

Right The ramp is easily large enough for the jumpers to come out in pairs in very short order

Like most aircraft in its class, twin turbo-props lift what is essentially a flying
PortaCabin

Right The steerable canopy in fact generates considerable lift as it is also an aerofoil. This gentleman has quite literally, and with great precision, posed for the camera

Above A stand-up landing is the form for these chaps, not the undignified rolling in the dirt that ordinary parachutists endure

Left But they can't escape the trudge back . . .

Above The other unusual pair at Fort Bragg are the Fokker F.27s belonging to the Army's parachute display team, the 'Golden Knights'. Made up of instructors, the Knights put on a remarkable display of precision parachuting that never fails to please the crowds

Right Sgt Doug Wayne brings the flag in to Pope's annual open day. Designed so that the families and local taxpayers can see what their servicemen and women do, the Open House is actually a large airshow, and quite unlike anything seen in Europe

Whilst 'Thunderbirds' ground crew feign nonchalance, the Army shows that it too knows a thing or three about precision

Ready for anything

Below The 82nd is its soldiers. This ferocious looking band lug a considerable amount of fire-power between them. From left to right, an M-249 SAW (Squad Automatic Weapon), which uses the same 5.56 mm ammunition as the standard M-16 rifle (just visible behind) and can be belt or magazine fed. Next, the classic 7.62 mm M-60 GPMG (General Purpose Machine Gun), an M-249 with a 22 round box, another 249, and finally an M-16A2 rifle with attached M-203 grenade launcher

Right The radio operator and other squad members await the arrival of the helicopters

Above A closer view of the M-203 grenade launcher

Above left An M-60 with its minders. Troopers in the 82nd may go into battle by air, but like all paratroopers around the world they are essentially foot-soldiers—albeit exceptionally good ones

Left Figuring more prominently in the personal kit of the modern soldier of the 1990s is the 9 mm pistol, a gun designed to replace the classic .45 as the standard issue individual weapon. Whilst lighter, and arguably more accurate than its famous predecessor, the 9 mm cannot stop trucks, a legendary feature of the .45

Above right In common with the new generation of American military aircraft, this individual relies on stealth for his survival. As with other US Army snipers, he has had to resort to an earlier generation of weapon, in this case the M-14, to obtain the necessary range and accuracy his profession demands. Modern assault rifles are close-range, small calibre weapons and are not suited to this type of work

Artillerymen form a defensive perimeter as firing is completed

The time has come the walrus said... of Humm Vee, Hemmett, and Sheridan

The 82nd uses an abundance of ancilliary equipment and vehicles, some old, some new, but all judged best suited to the Division's various roles. Perhaps the most demanding test placed upon a piece of equipment is its ability to withstand an airdrop during a mission. Here a Dragon team proves this point. Anti-armour weapons are of great importance to the lightly equipped paratroopers. The M-47 Dragon is now an old weapon but can be carried by a parachutist in the initial assault. Here, at the moment of firing, the distinctive back blast can be seen

Overleaf main picture The other major anti-armour weapon is the Tube-launched Optically-tracked Wire-guided (TOW) missile. This missile has a range of some 3000 metres, and, being wire-guided, is difficult to jam or deflect. Watched by a Dragon team, the HMMWV mounted TOW II missile has just left the launcher at near sonic speed trailing its two wires

Overleaf top If you've been wrestling with HMMWV, which of course stands for High Mobility Multipurpose Wheeled Vehicle, don't worry. The manufacturers call it the 'Hummer', but on Fort Bragg it seems to be universally known as the 'Humm Vee'. Replacing the M-151 'Mutt' (the last of which is already in the Division's museum), the 'Humm Vee' is truly ubiquitous, and possesses a remarkable cross-country ability

Overleaf bottom Spotted outside the Division headquarters, yet another 'Humm Vee' variant, the M-998 carrier

Below Resembling a scene reminscent of the Western Desert during World War 2, this is in fact DZ Sicily, Fort Bragg's major drop area

Left Another vehicle that is rapidly being replaced by the 'Humm Vee' is the Gamma Goat, this particular example belonging to a Guard Unit. Used in considerable numbers, it was designed as a light all-purpose load carrier

Left below Captured by stealth photographer and Army aviator Bryan Wilburn, this supplier to the military clearly knows who his prime customer is. Pictured outside the base PX, it is not clear whether this item of vital equipment would be deployed in the first wave. Delivery is believed to be by the LABES (Low Altitude Beer Extraction System) method

This is an Oshkosh 'Hemmett' which, like the 'Humm Vee', comes in a variety of forms, including a refuelling tanker. Illustrated is the M-985 cargo truck which is used to bring ammunition to forward areas. It has its own crane for handling palletised munitions, but here good old-fashioned muscle power is used to unload 2.75 in rockets at an Apache arming pad out on the ranges

Below Vulcan. Descended from the classic Gatling gun of the 19th century, this is a truly awesome weapon in operation. Capable of firing at 3000 rpm—that's 50 rounds a second—a burst has a very distinctive deep ripping sound, and a devastating effect on whatever it hits. Deployed in the Division primarily as an anti-aircraft weapon, it can also be used with considerable effect in the direct-fire role. Originally developed for fighter aircraft nearly three decades ago, this is the same gun that is used in the Phalanx shipboard anti-missile system, and in three-barrelled form, in the Cobra attack helicopter

Left Here, elevation and traverse are being checked during maintenance. Operationally, the whole Vulcan cannon is shrouded in camouflage and virtually invisible. This should result in passing enemy pilots having to report that they were shot down by a 20 mm shrub

Fort Bragg also hosts a large range of other soldiers such as ROTC and Guard units who use the facilities for their annual training. This M-110A1 8 in self-propelled howitzer belongs to C Battery/5th Btn 113th Field Artillery, a local unit of the National Guard

Just coming into service, the MLRS (Multiple Launch Rocket System) is a sophisticated rocket artillery system. Very accurate and capable of dispensing a number of sub-munitions like anti-tank mines, or guided sub-missiles, the weapon has a range of some 30 kilometres and packs quite a punch. Based on the same chassis as the Bradley armoured personnel carrier, it is fully mobile and air-transportable. MLRS is also the subject of a major NATO programme and is now entering service with the British Army

Unique to the 82nd is the M-551 Sheridan. The last unit to use it operationally (there are still a few disguised as Soviet types at the National Training Center), they keep it on because it's still the only tank that can be dropped out of a Hercules. Whilst they freely admit it's an 'old klunker', it does the job, is fully amphibious and air-droppable to boot. The most interesting feature of the Sheridan is its dual main armament. Operating as a conventional gun it fires 152 mm ammunition. This odd calibre resulted from it being designed around the MGM-57 Shillelagh missile, for which the gun barrel doubles as launch tube. The Shillelagh is now a 30 year old system which has theoretically been superceded by the TOW family of missiles. It can, nevertheless, give the newer missile a run for its money at the weapon's maximum range of 3000 metres

'Now for something completely different'. Three handsome shark-mouthed T-34C Turbo Mentors are operated as photo-chase aircraft by the Army Test Board on behalf of all services involved in the dropping of equipment from aircraft. They are, in fact, Navy airframes operated by the Army and flown from an Air Force base by civilians—which makes for some rather interesting paperwork. The unit flew T-28 Trojans in the past and is looking for a faster replacement for the T-34. The favoured type is the PC-9, although procurement might be a problem

Left Jim Isbell is one of three pilots in the unit who, between them, have amassed an impressive total of 22 years/30,000 hours accident free flying whilst engaged in test and evaluation work. Their total experience adds up to an amazing 75 years

Above The unit's aircraft are maintained in immaculate condition. For those interested the colour scheme is white and FS 12246 orange

Overleaf The unit patch is reproduced in full colour on the tail and beneath it is the abbreviated Navy BuNo indicating the airframe's original owners

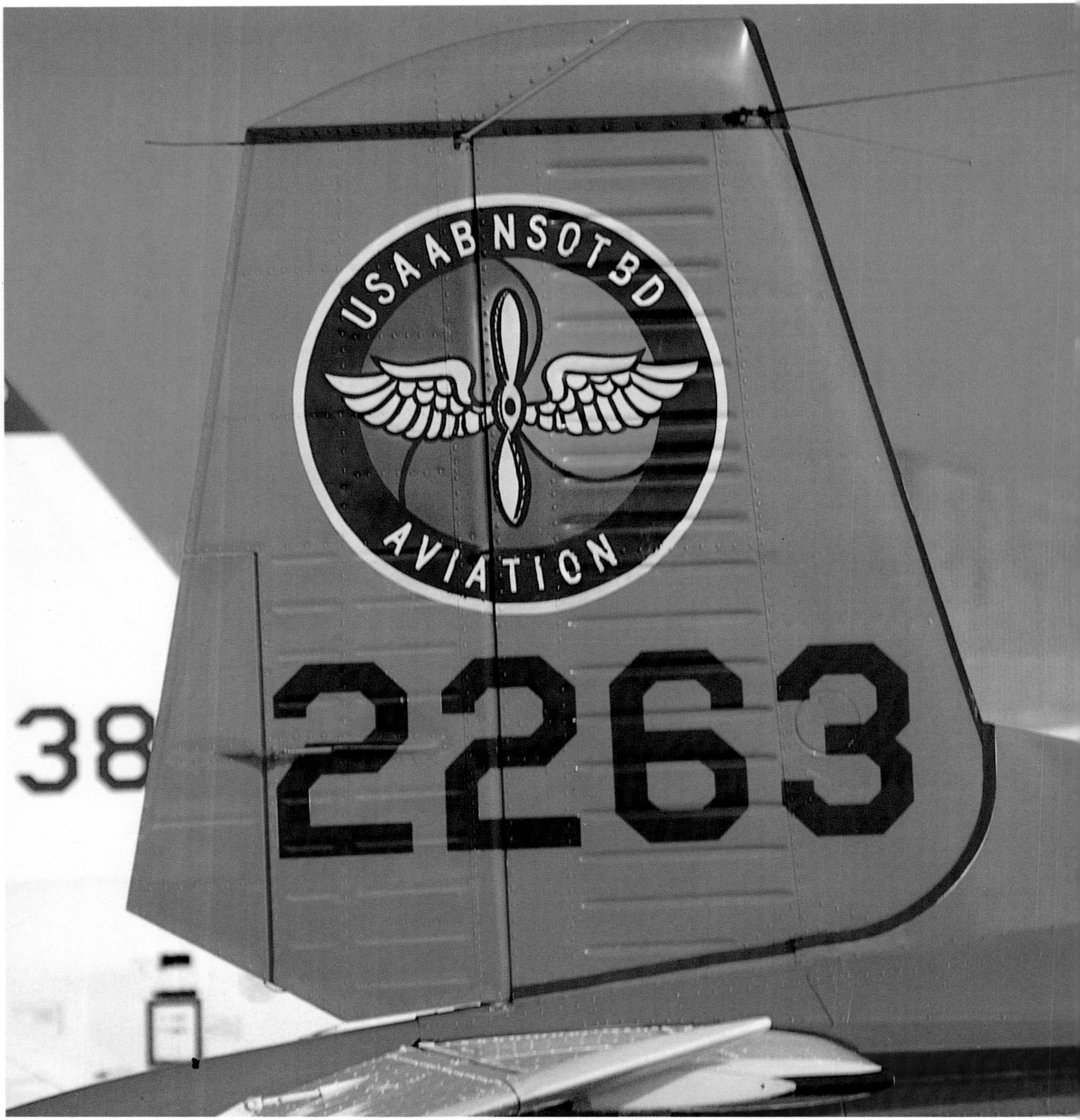
USAABNSOTBD
AVIATION
2263
38